WHEN TEARS FALL

An Autobiography

Verne Johnson

 authorHOUSE®

AuthorHouse™
1663 Liberty Drive
Bloomington, IN 47403
www.authorhouse.com
Phone: 1-800-839-8640

First published by AuthorHouse 10/15/2009

ISBN: 978-1-4490-1180-2 (sc)
ISBN: 978-1-4490-1181-9 (e)

Printed in the United States of America
Bloomington, Indiana

This book is printed on acid-free paper.

This book is dedicated to my two brothers,
Nate and Tyrone (Ghost). It is also dedicated
to all of my brothers and sisters who are either
struggling with addiction or who have with lost
their lives on the battlefield of their addiction.
To the families: be strong. Never lose hope.

THANK YOU

First of all, I would like to give thanks to my Father in heaven and His Son Jesus Christ for making it possible for me to live a productive and God-fearing life. I also give thanks to my beautiful and loving wife Stephanie Fusinetti-Johnson, who has believed in me from day one. I love you so much, baby, for being patient with me. It never went unnoticed. You have kept me strong when I wanted to give up on myself. You have loved me even when I did not think I was worthy enough to be loved. You are my rock!

To my adorable children LaVerne TayJuan Johnson III (Popi) and Celicia Nevaeh Johnson (Celie): you two are my life. I thank the Lord that He would entrust you guys to my care. Popi, you have been strong with me for ten of the twelve years that you have been in this world. Thank you, my son, for believing in your Dad even when times were very hard for us.

To my family: I hope I did not hurt or offend any of you by writing this book. You are all dear to me even if I do not show it all the time. Mama, I love you. Thank you for bringing me into this world.

To my best friend in the world, J.R. Riley. You are a true friend and brother. I remember when Nate died and you drove me to Subway to get something to eat because I had not eaten in days. On the way back to Mama's house, I broke down. You pulled into a parking lot so no one would see me crying. You put your arms around me and told me that I still had a brother in you. That was over ten years ago, and you have never wavered from that comment. Nate would be very proud of you for taking care of his BIG BROTHER (lol). I love you with all my heart. I will never forget that I've got you when I make it.

To my brothers and sisters in the struggle of drug addiction and alcoholism: never give up on yourself, no matter how tough things get. Give yourself at least one chance. To all of my friends past and present: you all have had something to do with who I am today, whether it was for good or bad.

Last but never least, my dear Granny, I miss you so much. I wish you were here to see the man I have become. Thank you for never giving up on me. I will see you after a while.

THE BEGINNING

I was born LaVerne W Johnson Jr. on May 22, 1975, in Rockford, Illinois, the child of LaVerne T Johnson Sr. and Noralynne Champion. I am a twin who came into this world ten minutes before my brother, Nathaniel Travirs Johnson. My mother, a short, dark-skinned lady about 5'4 in height, had my brother and I at the youthful age of eighteen. She did not know what to do with twin boys, being only eighteen and already the mother of a little girl, my sister Brenda. My grandmother tried desperately to keep Mama on the right track, but Mama did not want to do the right thing in life. Instead, she wanted to hang out with boys, partying, smoking weed, drinking alcohol, and coming home as she pleased. While she did her own thing out in the streets, she would keep the three of us at home with Granny, who lived in the Concord Common Projects. Eventually, Granny got tired of Mama's behavior and demanded that she move out on her own. In 1976, Mama got an apartment in the Organ Keys Projects where we would reside for over ten years. In those ten years, she would give birth to four more children, all of us with different daddies.

Mama, as I remember, was a very kind and loving woman. There wasn't anything she wouldn't do for Nate, Brenda, and me; she would do the best with what she had or was given. With the help of her very good friend TT, also a young mother with two sons, she raised us. Nate and I did not know our father. According to Mama, he was often in trouble with the law for crimes ranging from petty theft to drug selling. He and my mother had met in 1974, the year before my brother and I were born, in the Concord Common Projects. From what my mother has told me, my father was a "want-to-be" pimp. She said all of the girls desired him because he was so good-looking, with his light-skinned complexion, green eyes, and long straight hair. My mother said she was crazy about him, and she had to fight a lot of jealous girls just to keep him.

On the other hand, I never knew him. All I have are stories. The only time I remember seeing my father is when I was about five years old. He tried to break into our apartment in Organ Keys. Mama had told us to never open the door for anyone, and that night we did not, not even for my own dad. With my siblings and I looking out of the window, he threatened to "kick our asses" if we did not let him in. Now I cannot help but wonder how our lives would have changed if he were able to get into the house that night. I believe in my heart that he was probably a good man, but he played the hand he was dealt. His entire family was messed up with drugs, and they could not stand my mother, for reasons I do not know.

Growing up, I had to deal with some harsh sh*t. In 1977, when Nate and I were two years old, Mama was investigated by the Department of Children and Family Services (DCFS) because of complaints made by my paternal grandmother concerning Mama's treatment of us. This led to the worst thing that could have happened to Nate and me at the time—we were taken away from our mother.

In the three months that we lived in our paternal grandmother's home, we were treated like animals. Nate and I were beaten daily, called terrible names, and were not fed most of the time. While our grandma would be out running errands or shopping, my Uncle Tony, who was supposed to be watching us, would molest us.

He would make us do things to him while he watched television. Calling us "b*tches", he would tell my brother and I that we were "worthless" and "good-for-nothing." He forced us to walk around the house nude. He would also get my older cousin involved in molesting us. Often, Uncle Tony would tell me that he hated us and wished we would go back to our mother. I myself began to hate Mama for this; I felt she did not fight hard enough to get us home while we were living in that hell.

After much physical and mental abuse, Nate and I finally told Mama about the beatings, barely eating, and name-calling. We were too frightened to tell her about Uncle Tony molesting us because he had threatened to hurt us if we told anyone; he had also threatened that "the white man" would take us away from our mother. After what seemed to be an eternity, Nate and I were able to go back home because Mama got her house in order. She promised DCFS that she would keep the house clean and make sure that there was food in the kitchen at all times. In turn, the DCFS case worker told Mama that she could, and would, drop by the house at any time without informing her. I was glad to be at home, or so I thought. I did not think that living at home could be any worse than living at my grandmother's.

My step-dad Eli, who lived with our family from 1977 to 1986, was a monster! I hated him more than anything in this whole world! He was a coward. Mama was so afraid of him that she would let him do whatever we wanted to us. For no reason, this man would beat me on a daily basis; the beatings he gave me I would not give to my worst enemy. He would make me lie over the bathtub, my belly touching the top of the tub and my elbows touching the insides. When I was in this position, he ordered me to not move. If I moved, I would endure more hits. He would then take a two-by-four and strike my bare butt. I would use the bathroom on myself, and this would make him hit me even more. Truly, there were times that I just wanted to die!

I did not deserve half of the sh*t that this man did to me. I believe that he really hated kids, even though two of my siblings were his. When we would do something that he did not like, he would lock my brothers and me in a very small closet only big enough to hang a few coats. He called it "jail". I hated being in there! If I was in "jail," I could only come out to use the bathroom. If I was in" jail," I had to eat all meals there (that was if he did not forget about me). I could not go to school if I was in "jail". "Jail" was not a fun place to be, for roaches crawled on me, and even a mouse or two would make its way under the door. I could not scream or cry out loud, or I would get a beating. So many nights I wished for death to come, but I was afraid to die.

Not only would Eli incarcerate my siblings and me in our home, but he would deprive us of food, so we had to steal food from the kitchen. Many times we got caught, and the punishment was very harsh; the beatings were a hundred times worse than usual. I began to think about ways to kill Eli. Often, I wondered why this man would not just go to sleep and not wake up.

During this time, I did not understand my life. Mama was so terrified of Eli that she did not know what to do, and if she tried to help us out or tell him that that was enough with the beatings, he would get mad and beat her. Plenty of nights we would hear Mama get beat for no reason at all. This man was the devil himself! Sometimes now I feel that I still hate him. I can still see his face in my dreams. I can still remember the beatings. Even to this day when I see myself undressed, I am reminded of the pain he caused from the scars on my body.

One day I was in the utility room. The utility room was another room in our home that Eli had made a "jail". In this room were the washer and dryer hook ups, the hot water heater, and the furnace. There were also piles of dirty clothes all over the floor, which I would use to make a bed.

On this day, Granny came over to the apartment, and from the utility room, I could hear her talking to Mama in the kitchen. I heard Granny ask Mama if Eli was still beating her. Mama lied so very well. Granny then asked about her grandkids, and Mama continued to lie. I started faking a cough, just so I could let Granny know that I was in the utility room. She heard me. Mama quickly tried to lie, but it was too late. Mama said that it was "Eli's doing." She admitted to my grandmother that he was putting us kids in the utility room and the closet to punish us. Granny then began cursing at Mama. She told her to get her grandbaby "out of there" and to never put any of her grandchildren in there again. She stated that if it happened again, she would "kick" Eli's ass herself, and Granny did not play games. Eli would not cross the line when it came down to Granny.

The very next day the whole house was smoking. Unknowingly, a few hours earlier while sleeping, I had knocked off the cover from the water heater, and the utility room had caught fire. Granny had saved me from that fire.

I was always hoping my dad would come over to kill this coward. I came to hate my father for not being there, and for allowing this man to hurt me and my siblings at will. Why was no one trying to help us from this madness? Where were the police? Where was the rest of the family? Why were they letting this happen? Why was God allowing this to happen?

GROWING UP WITHOUT YOU

I was never the type who wanted my father in the stands watching me play some type of ball game. No, that was never my personality or style; I never liked to play sports, although I loved watching them on television. What I wanted was for my dad to teach me how to be a man. I wanted him to teach me how to survive out in the streets—basically, I wanted him to teach me how to be a reasonable human being.

I say this because all I had ever known in my youth was the street life. Like most of the kids I grew up around, I was raised in a fatherless home, but I was different from these kids: my father resided on Death Row in California's San Quentin Prison. When life would get difficult at home, despite Mama's best efforts at keeping the family together, I would often think of my father. My siblings and I had countless "step-daddies," none of whom we were ever able to call "Dad." While Granny was always there to pick up the pieces for Mama, it was not enough to make up for the absence of a true father in our home.

Particularly when we were living with Eli, I grew very afraid. I was terrified of him! I always wondered as he beat mom and us children how a man could do this to a woman and her family. How could a man say, "I love you," to a woman while keeping a straight face, and then turn around and slap her, or her child, in the face? I was very confused. If my biological father were here, I thought to myself, would he beat me like this? Would he beat my Mama like this?

I wondered, but I will never know because my father was not there. I wanted to ask my father, "Would you have hurt or killed the man who hurt your children? Where were you when we needed you to protect us from all the hurt, harm, and danger?" I sat many nights listening and comforting Mama as she cried because she needed someone to really love and help her. My father was not there, so I had to play the role of a man. I had to take on adult male responsibilities, and as a result, I grew up too soon.

Having spent most of my childhood living in fear and confusion because of the decisions my father had made, I came to wonder if he cared about Nate and me. Wanting to have a strong and wise man in my life, I turned to the gang chiefs. It was not only I who got involved with gangs; my entire family would become gang members, too. After all, we all had to learn the game of survival.

All I knew about my father was based on someone else's story. From others, I learned that he wanted to be promiscuous and that he "did not have time" for kids. There were allegations that he was a "murderer" and a "monster." People would tell me that my father "could not do anything right." Troubled by the stories I had heard about him, I desired to learn the truth from him. I wanted to know my father for myself, but he was not there. In his absence, I got involved with gangs, drugs, and alcohol at a very young age.

I am like most young black men who have grown up in the filthy streets of Rockford; we all share the same story. We have all heard terrible things about our fathers a thousand times over. At this time in my life, I want to reach out to those who have shared my fate. I want to talk about the pain, bitterness, sorrow, loneliness, lack of love, lack of knowing how to give or receive love—in short, the brokenness that we all share. We share a similar history, and in order for us to move forward into the future, we must confront our past. Personally, I have had to dig through the layers and layers of pain and meet it head-on. I have had to recall those things that nearly killed me a thousand times over. I have had to go to the men and women in my life and tell them how much they have hurt me; I have also had to allow them to tell me about the hurt that I have caused. At this time in my life, I cannot lie, sugar-coat, ignore, or withhold the truth.

INSIDE PAIN

Have you ever smashed your finger in a door or stubbed your toe on the edge of a bedpost? As the pain begins to surge up and down throughout your body, you want nothing more than for it to go away. You wait all the while, sweating, cursing and holding the area that is causing the throbbing pain, and most of the time, after a few minutes, the pain goes away.

Now imagine that this pain continues for five, ten, fifteen, or even twenty years, and you never take any medicine for it. Could you live with that?

My heart has lived with pain for years: I have felt great pain from my father not being a part of my life. In my youth, I had not been taught how to express my feelings in an appropriate manner, nor was I given the opportunity to confront the man who was causing me this internal pain. Eventually, my pain grew into bitterness, and then into hatred.

The first time I was given an opportunity to confront my father, I was seventeen years old. We had a phone conversation. During this conversation, we didn't actually talk—instead, we yelled and cursed each other out. I became very angry with him, and we did not solve anything in that fifteen minute exchange. When the phone minutes expired, the situation between us was as bad as it had always been. I did not know what to do. I remember feeling that I hated this man! He was not my father, and I knew absolutely nothing about him! So why was I angry with him?

In my heart, I had wanted him to be a father. I needed him to know how much I wanted him to be there for me. But I also had no respect for him, and I could not look up to him as a father figure. He was just a man who had helped my mother bring me into the world. I wanted to tell him all about myself, but I could not trust him.

After that phone conversation, we did not talk for six years. During that time, I figured it was up to him to pick up the phone or a pen to try to re-establish contact with me. After all, I reasoned, it was his fault that we were in this situation.

Later I would learn that it takes two to begin a relationship. In order for this to happen, both parties have to be involved, and both have to want the relationship. I did not want a relationship, but my father did. At the time, I wondered how it would be possible for me to have a relationship with a man that I hated so much, a man I did not know, nor wanted to know. Bitter in my heart, I felt that he owed me something. And I would ask myself, "What did my family and I do to deserve this?"

In the late 1980s, years before I was to have this encounter with my father, my Mama moved our family to Beloit, Wisconsin. During the time that we lived in Beloit, I had got so fed up with being the talk of the town and school that I wanted to kill myself.

Every day since childhood, it seemed, I had been forced to fight just because people did not like me. In Rockford while attending elementary school, I had no friends outside of my brother, Nate. Perhaps we were disliked because we did not have many clothes: my brothers and I had to share three shirts and two pairs of pants. I can recall feeling ecstatic to get my cousin's second-hand clothes and shoes, and even though they were too big for me, I wore them anyways. But by wearing them, I was talked about even more. Kids would call my siblings and I nasty names; one that stuck was the "Brady Bunch Chumps," given to us because there were seven of us.

When we would walk home from school, my brother and I had to fight nearly the entire walk home. Then, upon getting home, we had to fight with the kids in the projects. These kids would not leave us alone! Why did they think they were better than us? They lived in the projects just like us, and their mothers were also on welfare, but in their minds they were superior. I could not understand how they thought this.

Growing up, I was an ugly kid, not very good with the girls, and all the other kids made sure I knew it. Feeling pain and fear from being rejected, I started to live in a fantasy world. I did not know who I was or what I wanted out of life.

One thing I did know for certain, though, was that I was afraid to go home after school and get the ass beating that would be waiting for me because I had not cleaned the kitchen. Mama, I knew, would be waiting behind the door with the fan belt. Throughout my youth, Mama also beat me for any and every thing. I do not know if this was her way of showing love to me, or if she just hated having all of us kids. For a long time, I believed that she felt we had ruined her life by standing in the way of her dreams. Entering my teenage years, I was never treated with respect or love from her. "Why doesn't this woman love me?" I would ask myself. "I am her son. Why am I being called every name known to man, besides my birth name?"

I started to believe that I was never going to be sh*t in life. No one believed in me, except for my brothers. No one loved me but my brothers. We were so close! We were survivors.

We did not have a choice. We stole food for each other just so we could have a meal to eat. Most of the time, all we could get were a few candy bars. I became so fed up with this life that I turned to the gangs, and while I knew at the time that it was not the best decision, I was tired of getting my ass kicked on the streets and at home. I was tired of being a nobody and wanting so badly the approval of others in the hood and in school.

My best friend in Beloit, Charles, would tell me stories about some of the guys he was hanging out with. He said that they were really cool guys, and he told me about the girls and the parties that this one guy, Lord Rock, would be having at the parks.

I can remember one day while Charles was talking, just standing there, waiting to ask him where this guy was and how I could join his gang. I told Charles that I wanted to meet this guy. Then, a few days later, while my brother, Eli Jr., and I were at the park doing back flips, a light-skinned guy yelled out, "Hey, little man! Let me see that again."

There were many boys and girls around this man. I did not know at the time that he was Lord Rock, the guy Charles had talked about. Lord Rock called Eli and me over, and as I got closer, I saw Charles talking with two guys in the back of a car. I heard Charles say, "Yeah, man. This is the dude I was telling you about. He wants to be down with Vice Lord."

Lord Rock looked over at me. I was thinking that he was going to reject me also, but he just smiled, saying, "So you want to be a Lord?"

I had no idea what he was talking about. "Do I want to be what?"

"A Vice Lord," he said again.

I said, "Yeah, I will be a Vice Lord. What will I have to do?"

He told me that I had to be "blessed in." I asked him what that meant. He told me to meet him at the park the next day.

The next day I was not able to get to the park, for Mama had forbidden us to go outside because the house was a mess. Charles came over to get me, stating that Lord Rock was looking for me to show up at the park. I told Charles that Mama said we could not go outside; we had to clean the house. I then asked Charles if Lord Rock was angry with me. He told me "yes." He said that Lord Rock called me a "stupid ass nigga," and if I did not get with him by the next day, I could not join the gang, plus Lord Rock was going to kick my ass for wasting his time.

After that conversation, I made sure the whole house was clean so I could meet with Lord Rock and not get my face kicked in. At first, I was scared because I thought it would be like it was in the movies. I remembered the movie 'Bad Boys'--not the movie with Will Smith and Martin Lawrence, but the one with Sean Penn in a boy's locked-down facility. I thought of the Bloods and Crips street gangs in LA. I thought I would have to get beat up.

Fortunately, I was way off; I just had to say a few prayers and learn the literature that I was given. If I did not learn the literature by the next meeting, Lord Rock explained, then I would get the boot and a beat down.

For a week I studied my ass off, and by the next meeting I was able to spit all the material back at him. All the guys were amazed that I knew the literature in a week's time. Some were even jealous because Lord Rock was very impressed by my performance and had taken a liking to me. At that moment, at the age of twelve, I became a Vice Lord.

GANG LIFE

Becoming a Vice Lord was the best thing that ever happened to me. I was around kids just like me, kids who wanted to drop out of school because they got no respect, kids who were being raised in fatherless homes, kids who were living in the projects or in very bad neighborhoods, kids who were poor, kids whose mothers got high. I thought to myself, "What could be better than being around kids just like me?" We all had the same lack of morals and values; we just did not give a sh*t. Gang life was like a world set aside from the "real" world. We had our own kind of talk, walk, girls, blocks, families--we even had our own colors, and if people disrespected that, they got the beat down with no questions asked.

Back in the early to mid eighties, the only ones who were able to carry pistols were the gang leaders. Lord Rock had a twenty two automatic pistol, and he was not afraid to use it on anyone who got in his way or in the way of his members. I can recall a time when we were at the park and this guy, a Gangster Disciple (GD), had the nerve to call Lord Rock out for a fight. Lord Rock did not want to fight him because the guy was twice his size. As the guy got out of the car, Lord Rock pulled out his gun and shot at him. He did not actually hit the guy, but the sight was really funny--the guy took off running down the street so fast that he nearly beat the car that he had gotten out of. That was the first time other than on television that I had seen someone shot at.

The more I hung with the Vice Lords, the stronger I became. I had friends, friends who I believed loved me. Girls started to like me, too. I did not know if they liked me because I was in a gang or if they thought I was good-looking. I later discovered that it was neither of these things. Having friends and girlfriends just came with the territory.

The girls loved the way I would treat them. I was always kind to them, and I respected them. I never wanted to be like the men in my life, beating on girls, getting over on them by using them for money, sex, and their vehicles (if they had them). I treated the girls well, and they, in turn, gave me attention. Really loving their attention, I sought out their company. I loved to be around girls, and for the most part, they loved to be around me.

The first time I had sex, I was twelve years old. It was with one of my oldest sister's friends. I had no idea what to do; she did it all for me. I was so in love--not with her, but with sex. I loved having sex with her, even though while in the act I was troubled about my sexuality. I was afraid that I was a homosexual. Now, I do not believe that I was ever attracted to men, but when I was young, I felt like perhaps I was because of what my uncle Tony had done to me. He had taken so much from me: my innocence, my manhood, my self-esteem. Because of what I had experienced as a child, I tried to sleep with as many girls and women as I could. The only time I was not sleeping with a woman was when I was locked up in the county jail or in prison, but even then, I was still trying to hook up with female guards.

Being around girls in the gangs not only helped me build self-confidence, but it also helped me realize that I truly loved women. My first girlfriend was my next-door neighbor, Kenzi. Kenzi was ugly, but she had a sweet heart, and she loved me very much; we had a lot of fun together. Her mother and mine were friends. I loved it when our mothers would party all night because I knew that I would be with Kenzi. We talked all the time about life and what we wanted in life. I really thought I was going to be with her for a long time, and so did she. About two years later, she moved.

Not only did the girls help me to feel better about myself, but being around Lord Rock helped me, too. Lord Rock was the first man I had ever respected. He handled himself very well, and his clothes were always nice and clean. I never saw him wearing the same outfit twice, and his shoes were as white as snow. One thing I can say, though, is that while Lord Rock was the coolest guy that I had ever met, nothing in this world is for free-- not even a man's friendship. As a gang member, I had to put in work for the gang. I had to do things like steal from other gang members, breaking into their cars and houses. At the time, it did not matter to me because I would do anything for the Vice Lord Nation, and I mean anything.

After I had joined the Vice Lords, my friend, Charles, dropped out of school because school was getting in his way, taking time from him, time he believed he could be making money. Charles wanted to be a full-time drug dealer. At 13, he was probably one of the youngest guys in the hood who had his own car. He wore nice clothes and shoes. Charles was from Chicago and had two brothers, one older and the other younger. He and his brothers had grown up very fast.

One night when Charles and I were sitting on the porch, drinking some Mad Dog 20/20 we had stolen from the local grocery store earlier that day, I asked him how was he able to afford all of his nice clothes. He told me that he was selling dope for his oldest brother. I asked him if he was selling weed. He stated, "Yeah a little weed", and he then told me his big brother was "doing it big with powder cocaine."

I looked at him and said, "Man, you're pushing cocaine?"

He said, "What nigga, you got a problem with that?"

"No," I replied. "I do not have a problem with it, but aren't you scared?"

"See man, that's why your ass is broke," Charles said. "Look at you, your ass wearing the same sh*t Nate wore yesterday!"

I was pissed because he was right. I hated living and looking like a bum. I had nothing, and the little money I did have came from the block boys who loved to shoot craps. I was pretty good at shooting craps, but not good enough to make a living.

During this and subsequent conversations, I avoided telling Charles that my mother was selling more dope and making more money than his brother did. Cocaine was all around me, and I did not even know its value. Mama would wake me up in the middle of the night, high and paranoid that someone was going to rob or kill her. She would have me hide hundreds of dollars worth of cocaine in her maxi pad boxes. For months, I had observed my mother selling coke. I had watched her every move and transaction with dealers and with addicts.

I watched as the money exchanged from their hands to hers. The money was flowing so fast she did not know what to do with it. The more she made, the more she got high. I then started to take a few bags here and there. No one knew I was stealing bags of dope from Mama. I continued stealing until I had over $400 worth. I only knew the worth because later I took it to Charles for him to help me sell it. When he saw it, he could not believe it. He actually thought it was not real because it was more cocaine than he had ever seen. He opened a bag and tasted it.

I asked him, "Man, why are you putting that sh*t in your mouth? Your ass is going to be a dope fiend."

"Shut up," he said. "In order to see if it's real, you have to taste it. If it numbs your lips and tongue, it's real."

From that night on, Charles taught me all he knew about selling drugs. He knew that his brother could not compete with my mother; she had the whole city wrapped around her finger. I was getting as much cocaine as I needed for free, so he made sure no one was able to get close to me to find out about the dope I was taking from Mama. Charles instilled in me to never fear the dope game, or more particularly the individuals involved in the game. He stressed that the moment I became fearful, I would either get caught by the police or killed by a "nigga". I am not here to brag nor boast, but out of eleven and a half years of selling drugs, I was never caught or locked up for selling them, and I never told on anyone else who was selling them, either.

Mama never knew about me taking her dope. By the time I was fourteen, I was making so much money that I did not need to take dope from her anymore. I would only take it from her if I "fell off"—that is, if I had lost out on a drug deal gone bad or had no money to buy dope. At fourteen, I was completely financially independent. The money was coming in so fast that I decided we were going to need to hire more guys for protection, so Charles and I got a few of our young friends and put them on the payroll to work for us.

During this time, I did not trust anyone, and I would take all of my dope to school and hide it next to the dumpster. After a while, doing poorly at school and afraid that I might get caught with drugs on school property, I said to myself, "Forget school and all of the people that ever talked about you." At the age of fifteen, I dropped out of the ninth grade because I figured that school was doing nothing for me but getting in the way of my making money.

I was in control of my life, or so I thought. Lord Rock, who had found out that Charles and I were making lots of money selling drugs, was impressed with the crew I had put together. He even assigned a few guys to assist us just to ensure that his "cut" would not stop coming.

In the meantime, the small town of Beloit could not supply us with the dope that we needed to keep in business, so Charles would take us to Chicago to buy dope.

At thirteen, he was too young to have a driver's license, and there were no plates on his car, so we would take plates from cars in the parking lot of an apartment duplex down the street from my house. We did this many times, and we never got caught.

Driving to Chicago during this time was one of the best times of my life! Just the rush I got from doing whatever the hell I wanted was so cool! Going into the projects to buy dope was a grown up thing to do. It felt like we were in the big league--but being in the big leagues came with a price.

Guys started to plot against us, and Charles was robbed nearly every weekend. I was robbed a few times, too. Even our own Vice Lord Brothers "hated on" (betrayed) us. Also, the cocaine was getting weaker and weaker by the month. In order to make a few more dollars, the suppliers were "stepping on" the dope, diluting it with baking soda and Doan's back pills to the point where it was losing its potency. We needed to do something, and fast.

One morning in 1990, Charles came over to my house and told me about a call he had received from his cousin, who told him that we should come to Chicago and bring "lots of money"; his cousin was a dealer who had dope to sell. As we sat on the porch, we figured out how much money we had. At that time, I only had a few hundred dollars to my name, and Charles had a little over three hundred, so we had just over five hundred dollars between us. We were able to get more money from my brothers, who were also selling for another dealer. Later that night, we headed to Chicago with two other Vice Lord brothers, Shawn and Kenny, and two guns, just in case someone tried to rob us, for this was all the money that we had.

When we arrived in Chicago around 2 a.m., Charles' cousin was nowhere to be found, so we went to the projects where Charles had grown up. There Charles saw a guy walking by who knew his cousin, and the guy told us that Charles' cousin was a few blocks down the street in another building. Charles knew the place well, and when we got there, he asked us to wait in the car, but to keep the engine running. He also asked Shawn to go inside with him. About ten minutes later, Charles and Shawn came running back to the car, breathing heavily, and jumping into the car, they screamed to Kenny in the driver's seat, "Go! Go!"

We were all so scared! Charles was yelling at Shawn, calling him a "stupid m*therf*cker". Charles said that Shawn had almost got them killed. We were deep in GD territory, and Shawn had forgotten all about the five-point star cut into his head that read CVL (Conservative Vice Lord). The guys only let them go because one of them was a friend of Charles' cousin, and he knew Charles' family.

All I was worried about was the dope. In most cases, even if dealers have the heart to let you go, they still rob you. Fortunately for us, this was not the case.

Charles told us that they did not have any powder cocaine, so they gave him eight rocks in baggies. Each rock was about the size of a golf ball. According to Charles, the guy told him, "If you take this sh*t to your neighborhood dope heads, they are going to love your ass." At the time we knew nothing about crack cocaine. What we did know was that some of our customers would cook powder cocaine into a rock, or crack form, and smoke it, but because the powder was so stepped on with baking soda, they did not get much back to smoke.

We took that crack back to Beloit, and the dope game as we knew it was no longer the same. We called this dope "ready rocks" because addicts no longer had to cook it into rock form anymore. All they had to do was put it in their pipes and smoke it. Our customers would walk down the streets or drive their cars, and never again did they have to put up a spoon or mirror (both used to cook crack cocaine). Customers loved us, and the guys who were still selling powder cocaine could not figure out how we were taking their customers away from them. They would send people on our block to spy on us and report back what we were doing.

At this point in my life, the Vice Lords got very demanding of my time. I was the getaway driver in several multiple drive by shootings, and I was involved as well in beatings and robberies of other gang members and drug dealers. I did things to people that I hoped would never be done to me. Because I had to make Vice Lord business a priority, I could no longer make much money doing drug deals on the side.

With my deepening involvement in the Vice Lords came many trips to jail; I have spent more than half of my life in jail, sitting, doing nothing, wasting time when I could have been reaching positive goals. Going to jail became such a part of my life that I got to the point where it did not even bother me any longer, for I accepted it as a part of the gang lifestyle. However, there were times that I missed being at home with my family. Also, it was tough being in jail for none of my family or friends visited me or wrote letters. This made the time go by slowly.

In 1993, I was arrested and sent to prison in Green Bay, Wisconsin, for a mob action and drive by shooting. By the time the case was over, I had spent a little over two years in county jail and prison combined.

THE CAGE

Imagine that you live in a room the size of your bathroom, about five by ten feet, with someone of the same gender whom you do not know. The space has two bunks, one cupboard for each of you to store your property, and a metal toilet at one end of the bunks with a small sink beside it. The cell space is so small that it cannot accommodate both of you standing: one of you must always be sitting or lying on a bed. Also, you cannot sit up straight in either bed without bumping your head. Now visualize that you live in this room nearly twenty-three hours a day for weeks, months, or even years.

The only time it is silent is between the hours of 2:00 and 4:00 am. You never have space to yourself: you sleep, go to the bathroom, dress, eat, and fart in this room. Each morning you are awakened at 5:00 a.m. to eat breakfast with hundreds of other men. The food is often cold, with very little nutritional value. You have to use plastic utensils instead of real silverware—real knives could be used to hurt yourself or others.

After breakfast, you go to work for sixteen cents an hour, and while working you remember two friends who worked with you for months, the only guys you could be really cool with. One got transferred unexpectedly, and you never got to say goodbye; the other got stabbed in the basement. That is when you decide to never get close to anyone again.

Gradually, you begin to attend 12-step groups and church services. You play baseball and walk the yard. You are proud of yourself for the first time in your life, and you have earned the respect of others while "inside." You have also begun to realize that your drug and alcohol problems sit atop of a much deeper pain, and that the groups you now participate in might provide some healing for the rage that surfaces when you feel tense. For the first time in your life, you see the connection between the beatings your stepdad gave your mom, brothers, sisters, and yourself and the fury that can explode out of you like the fizz from a Coke that has been shaken vigorously. This insight gives you hope: one day, you think, you may be able to change.

Envision you have got only six months left in this place. Happiness and fear are competing inside of you. The thought of being free is so intense that you can almost taste it! What would it be like, you wonder, to just hang out with your homies again, get high, and have sex with the girls of the neighborhood? Aroused by an anticipation of freedom, you picture yourself getting up in the morning when you feel like it, and earning more than sixteen cents an hour at work. Yearning for freedom, you can see yourself doing simple things, like crossing the street, buying a drink, seeing your family, and smelling the night air.

And yet, in the midst of your imagining, you are scared, for you know that when you are released, you are going to have to walk through the prison gate with only a few hundred dollars in your pocket and the clothes on your back. You will be walking out with a felony record, and the only people who will still know you will be your Mom and brothers. You begin to fear that your parole officer will keep you on a tight restriction, and you worry that the stress may get to you. After all, it is a short ride back to prison should you turn to the relief of the sweet, mellow feeling taking drugs gives you. And yet who would not want that that smooth, energized, confident feeling? Who would not want to feel unafraid?

You must remind yourself that the choice to go back to drugs is nothing more than your one-way ticket back to the life you are trying to leave.

Imagine being told to find a job when you have nothing nice to wear to the interview, nor a home address or telephone number that you can give for people to reach you. Imagine, too, trying to begin and sustain an intimate relationship. Envision yourself trying to accept and love a person in a way you have never had a chance to learn, or to experience.

Imagine, too, trying to be cool about all of the changes that have occurred since you were last out on the streets.

Imagine that you are out of prison but that you are still afraid--afraid of the penitentiary that resides in your mind, a penitentiary that is, of course, totally portable.

I had to learn the hard way, for I spent most of my time as a youth in the penitentiary, planning how I could take over the drug game in my 'hood. Everything I had out there--money, drugs, cars, apartment buildings, girls, respect, even love--I had to count as a loss when I went away to prison. Being "in the game," I knew I had to leave it all behind. Being in prison or the county jail, a person learns not to hold onto the outside world. When I was released, nothing had changed inside of me, and I went right back to the streets. For most men, penitentiary doesn't rehabilitate them. Instead, it makes them better criminals.

My Addiction

The first time I took a drink was in 1987. I was twelve years old and with one of my mom's boyfriends. We were walking to his friend's house to do some work for him; he preferred to take me with him rather than Nate because I was not afraid to work. During our walk, we stopped at the store where he bought a few beers. It was hot outside, and yet he did not ask me if I wanted something to drink. I grew angry at him. When he opened one of the bottles, I asked him for a drink. At first he would not let me because he was afraid of Mama's reaction, but later he gave in, for I would not leave him alone. When we arrived at his buddy's house, I was drunk. I could not help him with the job, so instead he and his friend had me sleep it off.

I am not going to lie: I did not like to feel hung over, but I loved the way being drunk made me feel. Some of my friends would steal liquor from the local corner store, and we would drink it at a friend's house while skipping school; the friend's mother would not be at home because she worked the day shift. This lifestyle was not strange to me. On both sides of my family, there were addicts and alcoholics. I was used to this behavior, and I thought it was the right way to live. I could not see anything wrong with it. While growing up, we had parties every weekend. Mama was the party queen. Drinking was "nothing", she would tell us. She taught us that drinking was OK to do at home, but not out in the streets.

In the late 80's, Mama started using cocaine. Later, she started smoking crack. Having seen my mother overdose more than a dozen times, I vowed that I would never smoke crack. At first, I only drank, but later I started smoking weed. The first time I smoked weed, it was with Mama.

There was literally nothing that we could not do in Mama's house. At this point in her life, Mama did not care about us; we were all on our own. I was so stressed trying to take care of not only my siblings but Mama herself, that I would get high in order to escape the pressure. Drinking alcohol and taking drugs would just melt the stress away. Like drinking, it was never considered wrong to use drugs in our house, but if we used drugs outside on the streets, it was wrong.

As my siblings grew older, they began to do their own thing, and eventually most of us lost respect for Mama. For my part, I looked at her as just another crack head that I loved. Sometimes I would feel guilty about her being a single mother raising, or at least trying to raise, seven kids. "Does she have an excuse to live this way?" I would ask myself. I still ask myself that question. Maybe she did.

In 1990, Mama moved back to Rockford, leaving my oldest sister Brenda in charge of the family. In Mama's eyes, Brenda was old enough to look after the little ones. In the meantime, the rest of us did what we had to do to survive in the streets. The drug dealing never stopped; this was the only way we could pay the bills.

Later in the same year, the Beloit Gang and Drug Task Force raided our house. I was never in a raid before, and I was so scared that I pissed on myself. I remember lying on the couch and hearing this loud banging on the door--I thought it was someone coming to kill us. Men came in through the door with guns drawn, pointing them at my head. One officer pulled me by the collar of my shirt and threw me to the floor. Meanwhile, Brenda was trying to gather us all together, but the officers would not let her do this. After the raid, finding only paraphernalia inside the house, they told us that they knew we had converted the house into a drug house; they had been watching us for months. One officer made my sister give him the number to my mom's phone; he then called Mama, lying to her that one of her kids was hurt in an accident. Mama drove to Beloit and was arrested on the spot because the house was in her name. We all went to jail except for my baby brother and sister. My twin brother Nate was already in jail for another crime.

The detective let everyone go except for Mama and me; she was charged with running a drug house and spent over a year in the county jail. On the other hand, I was released after a few weeks. I went back to the house to get the money that I was hiding on the outside of the house. I would hide my money this way because I felt if a raid took place or someone came in to rob us, the money would never be found.

When I got home, my grandmother and sister Brenda were already there. The police were making all of us go back to Rockford to live with Granny. I decided right then and there that I could not do this. I had too much dope on the streets; there was way too much at risk. My boys needed me to be on the streets, I told myself. Determined not to go back to Rockford, I lied to my grandmother that I had to go pick up some money before we left. She knew that I was selling and using drugs, but she did not try to stop me. I then called one of my friends to pick me up at the corner store. He did, and we headed to Janesville, Wisconsin, that night.

Charles--not my former best friend but another Charles, whom I will call Chuck-- was older than me by four years. Chuck had a girlfriend who lived in Janesville in her own apartment; he told me that I could stay with them for a while if I would help him make some money. I told him that was cool, but after I met his girlfriend, I overheard her tell Chuck that her house wasn't a "daycare center." Chuck's girlfriend did not like me at first, so I would sleep in the empty apartment across the hall in an attempt to stay out of her way. After a while, though, we became cool with each other.

At this time, I started going out with a girl named Kerri. Her family did not like me because I was black; in fact, no one in Janesville really liked me. The white people did not like me because I was black, the GDs did not like me because I was a Vice Lord, and most of the guys did not care for me because I would be trying to take their girls. I was always fighting with some guy at the local club. Chuck would help me fight if the guy were older than me, but I was not afraid to stand up for myself and fight. I knew I was all alone, no matter who I was hanging with. I understood that I had to look out for myself.

Living in Janesville got better as time went on. I was there for about a year, and I never told my family that I was living there. They eventually found out from a guy that I partied with; he told Brenda, and she told him to give me her number if he ran across me again. I later called Brenda to find out that she was about $30,000 richer from a settlement she had won. She had bought her own place and wanted to see me, so my friends Kerri, Crystal, and Percy drove me to Rockford.

When I walked into my sister's home, I could see that she had it made, for she had set out for us all the dope and alcohol we could consume. Soon after this visit, my addiction for drugs, alcohol, women, and money reached its peak. I became completely out of control, leaving Janesville to move back to Rockford in 1992 where I formed a group of guys; the drug game was now even greater than before I had left. Brenda said she would help me "get back on" if I came home, and she did. Nothing and no one could stop me now; I had men and women working for me, and I was going to the top.

My brothers Nate and Eli Jr. joined me, and we made money. Drinking and drug use, however, became a big problem for us, and I began to slip and get careless with my crew and business. Even guys in my own gang began planning to rob me. They wanted me to fall.

I recall one night when my boys and I were invited to a party at the Rockford College Campus. We had called the girls we would be with on a time that we should arrive. They told us to meet them in an hour, so we decided to wait that hour at the local game factory. After a half an hour of playing games, I got a page from my half brother Tommy. At first, I ignored the page, but the pages kept coming. I had a friend call Tommy on an outside pay phone, and minutes later my friend came running back, saying, "Let's go! They just robbed your house and shot Tommy!"

Within minutes, we were all at the house. It was not a pretty sight. Everything that could be taken was taken, including my safe, guns, jewelry, and drugs. There were bullet holes throughout the entire back end of the house. Tommy had been in the bathroom, and there were bullet holes in the bathroom door; the intruders had been trying to kill him, thinking it was me. My only concern at the time was my brother. I would later find out that he had escaped through the bathroom window.

Extremely pissed at what I saw, I asked myself, "How could this happen? How could this happen when I have all this damn security!" I had been paying these guys good money to keep me safe. Needless to say, my security got dealt with in a very serious manner. I did not personally kill any of them, but I had one guy shot because he could not shut his mouth. At the time of the shooting, I did not care, for I had no feelings in my heart; the drugs and alcohol had made me heartless.

After this incident, I started taking vicodin and oxycontin to relieve myself of the pain and hurt that overwhelmed me. Running from myself, I made sure that no one in my gang knew that I was addicted to pain killers. Getting high on more than weed or alcohol was unacceptable in the gang.

BABY MAMA

In January of 1994, I met Jessica through a friend that I hung with in Rockford. Ray was a petty drug dealer, but he had a way with the ladies; also, his mother had a lot of money from a law suit she had won the year before. Ray spent most of his money on girls and partying, and when I met him, he was a few dollars away from being homeless. Nate and I were already homeless, living in a four-door 1988 Cutlass Supreme, with barely enough money for gas. We had to eat at McDonald's every day because it was the only thing we could afford, and we took bird baths at the local gas station, all of which got very old. We needed a place to keep ourselves up. One night, Ray asked Nate and I to give him a ride to a party at this girl Jessica's house; he also asked us to bring liquor and weed. I told Ray not to tell anyone that we were living in our car.

Ray agreed, and off we went. At the party, there weren't that many people there, just a few of Jessica's friends. That night I found out that Jessica had a six month old son and a very pretty friend, Kim, who was her roommate. Nate fell head over heels for Kim, and Kim didn't think he was too bad either, but who knows? Maybe it was the alcohol and weed talking.

Jessica and Kim loved hanging out with us; they thought we were really cool guys. At first, I didn't really like Jessica, and I wanted to go after Kim instead, but Nate had already called it. A few months after the party, my sister Sámi , who got high and drunk with us on weekends, told Kim that we were living in our car. Feeling bad for us, Kim and Jessica let us move in with them under the condition that we help pay the bills.

Jessica was behind on the bills because her mother had died six months earlier, leaving her the house; Jessica was only sixteen at the time. As for my brother and I, living in the car made it difficult to sell drugs, but when we moved in with Jessica and Kim, we were able to resume our business.

During the time that we lived with the girls, Jessica and I did not have strong feelings for each other. She said she just wanted to be friends, and so did I. We didn't even have sex with each other during this time.

Then in the spring of 1995, I went to county jail on a weapons charge, and shortly after that, Nate was locked up for a parole violation. While Nate and I were in jail, our brother Eli was doing big business selling marijuana in the Organ Keys Projects. One day in March of 1996, three months after I had been released from jail, Eli asked me to go to the projects with him to pick up a couple pounds of marijuana. While sitting in the car, I looked across the street and saw two girls outside talking; one looked just like Jessica, but it was too dark to tell. When Eli returned to the car, I asked him who the girls were. He said that one girl I had dated before going to jail.

"Who?" I asked Eli, looking again at the girls. "Jessica?"

"Yes," he answered.

I told him to "hold on", and he replied that he had two pounds of weed and couldn't sit around waiting because the projects were "hot."

"Then go do what you have to do and come for me later," I told him. I then got out of the car and ran across the street, calling out, "Jessica!"

Jessica looked over to see who was calling her name. "Oh my god! Verne?" she stammered, confused and surprised by my presence.

We talked the whole night; she told me that she was dancing at the Surf Lounge a local strip club. We had some good sex for the first time, too—I was fresh out of jail and needed it badly. Afterwards, she told me that she was involved with this guy who was a GD. I didn't really know him, but I knew of him--he was a chump and a woman abuser. Jessica told me that he was "crazy" and abused her.

"Kick him to the curb. I'll look out for you," I told her.

As it turned out, she was afraid to leave him. Also, she was using coke--something she claimed she would never do. From the looks of it, she was using it quite heavily. When I asked her why she started using coke, she stated that it was the only way she could dance in front of all those "nasty, heartless" men.

Over the next few months, I would go over to Jessica's house, not only to have sex with her but to see what she and her son needed. The guy she was with wouldn't do anything for her, Jessica told me; he would take all of her money and spend it on other girls, as well as on his boys. I was making a lot of money at the time, and my block was so hot that I needed a new place to sell drugs. Jessica's place was in the projects: it was the perfect place to set up operation.

However, I could not just take over her house by force-- I had to work my way in--and that I did. I let Jessica know that I was willing to put a real "hurting," or beating, on this guy if he got in the way of my making money, and Jessica asked me to do it "the right way" so I would not get caught. She had seen the money I was making and the guys I had on my payroll, guys who would ride with me all the way, and she was falling for me.

In the fall of 1996, after I had finished a few months in the county jail, Jessica asked me to move in with her. She lived in the front end of the Organ Keys Projects, so I set out to take over the entire front end. My brother Eli took over the back end where Mama was staying. Life was good: I was selling crack "up front" and Eli was selling weed "down low." I was back at last in the drug game, and we had not only the projects running but two drug houses on the southeast side of Rockford.

One night, my family, friends, and I were at the local club when this guy I knew out in the streets as an "off brand ass" Vice Lord--a guy not true to himself or the Vice Lord Nation--began to touch Jessica on her butt. She came to me several times about this matter, but I was so full of pills and liquor that I blew her off. Finally, the last time Jessica complained, I got up from my seat and went to the guy. I told him that Jessica was with me, and

I asked him to "respect my shit." He stated that he was sorry, but as soon as he said this, I knew he did not mean it, for he had to have already known that Jessica was with me.

Shortly after I went back to my table, Jessica and my sister Sámi came over to complain that "this punk ass nigga" couldn't keep his hands to himself. I walked to the dance floor, ready to knock his teeth through his jaws; he then pulled out a 9mm handgun. I looked down at the barrel of his gun, not fearing it; this was not the first time I had had a gun pulled on me. People started screaming and running, and I yelled out, "Don't run! This coward ass nigga don't have the heart or balls to shoot me in this club."

By that time, my boys got word of what was happening, and they were waiting at the other side of the club, with Nate going out the back door to get the gun from the trunk of our car. We wanted to kill this guy, for we knew he had made a big mistake: growing up in the streets, we were all told to NEVER pull a gun out on someone unless we planned on using it. That is Street Knowledge 101, and I had always played by the rules of the streets. Fortunately for the guy, he was able to make it out of the club by the time the police came. I, in turn, told the cops that nothing had happened because I wanted to kill the guy myself.

During this time in my life, Jessica was a "stand up girl": she was "down" with me, willing to do anything I asked of her. However, we had a very dysfunctional relationship. While we both accepted what the other was doing--I was okay with her dancing, and she was okay with my lifestyle in the streets—I realized that this was not the Jessica I had met years earlier. Her use of drugs had really changed her. Also, I would bet my life that she probably thought the same about me. Even our friends thought we were crazy for being with each other.

In the summer of 1996, a man was killed in the projects, and my brother Eli was blamed for it, but the detective could not prove that it was him, so the case went unsolved. The guy's brothers, friends, and family were angry about his murder, and the word on the streets was that one of his brothers was going to kill one of Eli's brothers. The intensity was overwhelming, and yet I can truly say that I was never afraid at this time; living with Eli Sr. as a child had taught me never to be fearful of any man again. Still, some of the very guys I hung with were trying to set me up: they would tell guys in the opposite gang where I was laying my head to rest. It was clear that guys in my own gang didn't want my brothers and I around any longer. Eventually, I went to Jessica to ask if she would have a baby for me; I was afraid of dying in this world and leaving nothing and no one behind. I wanted a child to carry my name. She agreed, and on September 16th, 1997, LaVerne (Popi) Johnson was born.

Until my son's birth, I had never thought life could be so precious, but when Popi was born, he became my life. Unfortunately, having him didn't really change me on the inside; I told myself that I had too much in the streets to lose. Nate was selling drugs for a very wealthy man, and he wanted me to come in on it with him. I agreed to work with Nate, only because I had robbing this guy in mind.

At this point in my life, I had no love for anyone in the streets: if you were not family, I was looking for ways to lay you on your back. I particularly hated the guys in the streets who thought they were tough but who were nothing but cowards. These guys thought that because they had money, they could buy muscle.

When Nate introduced me to his crew, I thought they were "weak ass": some of them were GDs while others were in the drug game for the first time in their lives. It seemed so unorganized that I wanted to slap them all, but then Nate told me that they were pulling in $70,000 a week. I did not believe him at first, so he allowed me to sit "on the blocks" (the neighborhoods) and watch the money come in. It came in so quickly that it was scary. There were seven dope houses, all running 24/7, and there were 17 workers, both male and female; it looked like a scene from the movies! I was impressed with what I saw and wanted badly to work with these guys—besides, I thought, who else was going to protect my twin brother?

Around this time, Jessica decided that she did not want to be a mother any longer. She was tired of staying at home with two little boys, so I moved her and the boys out of the projects into a nice apartment on 7th Street. Still she was not happy. Wanting to be back in the streets, she would call me, telling me that I needed to find someone to baby sit. When I declined, she would take her son to her brother's house and drop off our son at the dope house. This would force me to go home because I would not allow Popi to be at a dope house; he was only two months old.

I needed to be out in the streets, but having to watch my son kept me from making money. It was hard to find someone else to look after him because most of my family was in the streets as well. Still, I was determined not to let anything come between me and the money I needed to be making. Selling drugs was the only way I had to support Popi and myself and to pay the bills.

Actually, my brothers and I were making more money than we had ever made before. Feeling greedy, I told myself that I needed to be rich! I needed to have power! The guys I worked with meant nothing to me. I could easily take from them because I had no respect for them. I badly wanted to rob the head guy, but Nate asked me not to, reminding me that it was he who brought me into the business, and if I screwed him over, he would never forgive me.

In the meantime, Jessica decided that she was going to do her own thing; she was sick of me being with all kinds of women, spending entire nights out of the house, and showing no respect for her feelings. Generally speaking, I came home high 98 percent of the time, and it didn't matter to me what happened between us; after all, I had got what I wanted from her, a son. In all my time with Jessica, I never thought that she was a girl who would "settle down"; she just made babies.

When I found out from a buddy next door that Jessica was in our apartment one night having sex with one of the guys I worked with, I decided that she had to go. My buddy had told me that the guy's car was in front of the house all night. Instead of admitting this, Jessica lied over and over about it. I then asked her how she could have sex with another man in our bed—for me, that was the lowest of lows. When she did nothing but laugh in my face, it took every fiber of goodness in me not to grab her by the neck and throw her from the top balcony. Resisting the temptation to hurt her, I asked her to leave. Jessica then grabbed some clothes and yelled out, "I'll be back for the rest of my sh*t ,you f*uck*ing asshole!" When she walked out of the house, I just smiled.

After Jessica left in April of 1998, I moved my sister Sámi into the house with me, for she had a baby, too. Sami would work the block in the daytime and I at night. This worked out well for both of us; Sami had a baby-sitter during the day and I during the night.

Jessica came back to the house a month after Popi's first birthday in September. She was very high. She tried to kick the door down when she saw a woman walking to the bathroom. I called both Jessica's sister-in-law and the cops to remove her from my place. Later, I would learn from her brother that she tried to kill herself. According to Jessica's brother, a guy had found her unconscious on the streets and called for help.

When Jessica's brother and I spoke, Jessica was in the hospital and had asked to see Popi. Not wanting my son to see his mother in that condition, I declined her request. I did tell her brother that after she got out of the hospital, she could come to see him, but she never came by. Her brother explained that she felt it was best if she did not come around for a while.

It has been six years since I have seen or heard from Jessica. She was given my address and phone number, and Popi even wrote to her a few times, but he never got a letter in return. The day that Popi came to me, wanting to know why his mother did not love him, was very hard for me. It brought tears to my eyes. I told him that it had nothing to do with him, and that his mother was going through some issues that grownups go through. Of course, he asked, "Like what?"

I promised that I would tell him when he was old enough to understand.

PART OF ME DIED

On Sunday, October 11, 1998, Nathaniel Travirs Johnson, 23, of Rockford, IL, departed this earthly life at Swedish American Hospital as a result of an automobile accident. He was born May 22, 1975, the son of Noralynne Champion and LaVerne Johnson Sr. This day changed my life forever.

The night before his death was a night we all could not wait to see. This night marked the release of a new album. The album's artist, Sir Dragon, was my baby sister's son's father, and the entire family had VIP seats to the show at the local club, Lamont's. Setting out to be the best-dressed guys that night, Nate and I had shopped at the mall all day, looking for the perfect suit, which we found: a three-piece navy blue pin stripe suit with an eggshell color shirt and hat to match. We even bought matching navy blue shoes. I took my video camera to record the events of both that day and night.

On Saturday morning before we had gone to the mall, Tyrone, or "Ghost", a kid my mother had taken into her home, was acting as if he didn't want to come out with us that evening. He stated that he "don't f*ck with them niggas like that." Ghost hung with us until three in the afternoon, and once he left, Nate and I went out to eat at a local restaurant. In our conversation at the restaurant, we both decided that we were going to spend $1500 for the night's festivities; we also discussed what girls were pretty enough to spend the evening with us. From the restaurant, we called friends to tell them about the release party at Lamont's.

Once Nate and I left the restaurant, we drove to the mall, and it wasn't until we arrived at the mall that we decided to dress alike. In retrospect, it seems funny now that we had both agreed to do this: the last time we were dressed alike, our Mama was still lying out our clothes. After shopping at the mall, we stopped by our dope houses to both pick up money and drop off enough dope to hold the workers over for the night. Then back at the house we drank a bit with friends; among those friends were the girls who were going to hang out with us that night.

Nate's good friend J.R. called, wanting to join us, and we felt "the more the better." After we got dressed, I had the video rolling to record our arrival at the club. There were many people there, all looking to have a wonderful time, and that we did.

Around 1:30 am Sunday, family and friends who had gathered together around our table at Lamont's decided that we would go out to the Organ Keys Projects for an after party. As we left the club, though, Sámi and her boyfriend got into an argument, and the boyfriend decided that he was going to walk to the projects. I tried to get Sámi to ride with me in my car, but she refused and started walking after her boyfriend. Nate and I both yelled at her to get into the car, with Nate yelling, "F*ck him, Sámi! If you don't get into the car, I'm going to kick his ass." Still, Sámi continued to follow her boyfriend. It was nearly 2:00 a.m. and we were ready to leave the boyfriend, but we were not going to leave our sister in the streets that late. Because she would not leave without him, we threatened to kick the boyfriend's ass if he did not get into the car. After about thirty minutes, the boyfriend relented. We were all very high, and we just wanted to get to our destination.

On our way to the projects, it seemed like we were the only ones on the streets. Nate was in the front car, accompanied by three girls; I was driving behind him with Starr, Sámi, and her boyfriend; and J.R was driving behind me. In the car, I had been arguing with Starr about some girl who was all over me at the club; Starr didn't like it, so she had plenty to say about it. Sámi and her boyfriend were arguing also. In the meantime, Nate's car was way ahead of us, so I sped up to catch him; I was driving about 70 mph. Approaching the intersection of Harrison Ave and Kishwaukee, I glimpsed a red car to my left, but before I could say or do anything, Nate's car was hit. It looked like a scene from a movie. I was in complete disbelief.

From the car, Starr yelled, "That was Nate!", and then it struck me that this was my brother who had been hit. It did not look that bad until we got close to the car. Only then could we see that not only was there was no movement inside the car, but the engine had caught fire. J.R screamed that we had to get everyone out before the car blew up.

The girl who had been sitting behind the passenger seat was able to get out on her own, but her sister in the passenger seat needed help, for she was unconscious. Nate was slumped over the shift stick, not moving at all. J.R pulled Nate through the passenger side door and laid him on the ground; J.R, Sámi, and I then started to perform CPR on him, trying to restore his breathing.

The girl who had been sitting behind Nate was already dead. Terrified, Starr ran down the street to get Mama as we were only a few blocks from the projects. I was sitting on the ground in this empty parking lot, holding Nate in my arms, asking him to just hold on and stay with us. I kept telling him, "You're going to be fine." My brother took a deep breath, and then there was nothing but silence. It was 3 a.m.—only an hour after we had left Lamont's.

A few minutes later, I saw Mama running down the street, yelling, "What happened?" Someone—I don't remember who--grabbed her, and from my position on the ground, I could hear her screaming "Was that Nate? Was that my son?" I also remember J.R driving me to the hospital and telling me that everything was okay, but I didn't believe him. I thought my brother, who had been taken by ambulance to Swedish American Hospital, had died in the parking lot, but in my heart I still hoped that he was alive.

Once we got to the hospital, I saw so many people there that I wondered how the word had gotten out so quickly. Then after some time had passed, I heard my mother let out a scream I had never heard from her before. Hearing her scream, I realized that everything transpiring before my eyes was all too real--Nate hadn't made it.

Processing in my mind the fact that my brother was dead, I felt that I was losing my sanity--I couldn't imagine life without my brother, my twin! I asked to see Nate alone; I didn't want anyone with me. A police officer escorted me to the back room of the hospital, and entering this room, I saw what I did not want to see. There my brother lay--cold, naked, and lifeless.

I couldn't believe it--this couldn't be happening to me! I was going to wake up any minute! I walked over to my brother and looked into his eyes: they had turned a mild grayish color. There was a plastic tube coming from his mouth. Grabbing his body, I sobbed all over him, begging him to get up. As I cried, hugging my brother's body to mine, our lives together began to flash before me. I was missing Nate already, for I was thinking of all the things that I did not get a chance to say to him. After a while, I became conscious of the fact that the officer would ask me to leave, and I tried to collect all my memories. Then, losing all self control, I sank to my hands and knees on the hospital floor, crying out to God, "Why?" The officer came over to pick me up from the floor, and tears from his eyes splashed onto my face.

Not only did I lose Nate on this Sunday in October, but a few months earlier, in August, I had lost my brother Eli as well when he was sentenced to one hundred years in Joliet's Statesville Prison. The reality of losing two brothers was just too much for me to bear. My brothers had meant the world to me; I would have easily given my own life so that Nate could live and Eli be a free man again. Feeling unable to cope with my pain, on the morning of Nate's death, I thought about how I would take my own life. I had a 38 handgun. Also, my son was in Chicago with his mother at the time; if I did it now, I told myself, Popi would be too young to remember me.

Resolved to kill myself, I drove to the store, bought a fifth of Hennessey, and drove back home. Walking into my bedroom, I grabbed my gun and sat at the kitchen table, drinking the fifth until it was nearly gone. Still I could not do it. Crying out of anger, I asked myself, "Why! Why! Why! Why should I live?" I could only find reasons to kill myself. Then, in rage and despair, I started yelling at God, "You did this! Just take me, too! Why did you leave me here?" I wanted to be with Nate so very badly, and I continued drinking, crying, and yelling. I asked God to give me just one reason why I shouldn't kill myself.

Moments later, an image of Popi floated towards me, and in my head I heard, "That's your reason." The next day I could feel Sámi trying to wake me up from the table. She had called Mama to tell her that she thought I was going to kill myself because she had seen the gun in my hand, and the door was wide open. The police were called, and when they came, they tried to get me to go to the hospital, but I wouldn't go--I was afraid they would put me in the nut ward. Instead, I left the house, got into my car, and drove around town; the police followed me everywhere I went. My uncle Jimmy was able to convince me to come back home after nearly thirty calls on my cell phone.

On the afternoon of the next day, Monday, October 12, I called Jessica in Chicago to tell her the news and to ask her to come to Rockford to get Popi. She did not believe me at first, but after a few minutes she knew I was not joking. Jessica came to Rockford that morning, and she also attended the funeral that was held that Saturday, October 17, at St. Luke Miracle Temple in Rockford, which I thought was pretty cool, considering the circumstances. Even now, I feel it was for the best that after the funeral she took our son to stay with her; I really could not focus on a child at this time.

I had been asked to give the eulogy at Nate's funeral, but to tell the truth, when I delivered the eulogy, I had no idea of what the hell I was talking about. There were many people in attendance—some were Nate's enemies, and some were the guys we hung out with who only acted as if they were his friends. Others in attendance were the girls that he had slept with, including the mothers of his three sons. I started to wonder if most came because he was finally dead. His children's mothers looked both angry and sad, and I wanted to tell them that Nate's children were truly his life: he took care of them to the best of his ability, and he loved them very, very much. When he was alive, he would often say that he wished he could be with all of his sons, all of them living together, sharing a good life. I believe that before he died, he was trying to make enough money so that he could get out of the dope game and fulfill his dream.

After the funeral, we all went back to Mama's house, and low and behold this fucking coward was sitting in my mother's kitchen. Eli Sr., punk ass--I couldn't believe my eyes! This man had the nerve to enter into my mother's house after all the pain he put us through. I could see nothing but red--I was going to kill this coward!

I asked Mama, "What in the hell is *he* doing here? He has no right to be here!"

Mama responded in a soft voice, "He just come over for a short time."

I couldn't take it: I called him a "fucking bitch", and he said something nasty back. I then strode to my mother's room upstairs and grabbed my Glock 40. As I was about to leave her bedroom, Mama was standing at the door.

"Move!" I told her. "I'm going to kill this bitch!"

She begged, "Son, please don't do it! I can't afford to lose another son! Nate and Eli Jr. are gone; he's not worth the bullet!"

After my brother died, I entered the most painful period of my life. Those were my darkest days--days where I felt no hope or peace or life inside of me. Extremely depressed, I stopped eating and began using drugs and alcohol heavily. Consequently, I lost a lot of weight. Truly, I wanted to die, for I felt that my life was over. Also, I wanted to hurt whoever had ever caused harm to Nate, for I needed someone to pay for my loss.

During this time, I felt that my life was slipping away, and fast. Fortunately for me, Granny was very supportive; if not for her, I would not have survived this terrible time. She was the only one I felt that I could trust. Granny told me that God would take away all my pain if I would only turn it over to Him. I wanted to believe her, but I had never seen God help my family or me before. I asked her why God wanted to take my brothers from me. She answered, "Baby, God did not take your brothers. The lifestyle and those streets took your brothers." I would not understand her words until many years later.

Although I could not take care of Popi in the state that I was in, I needed to see him, so my friend Randy would drive me to the house that he and Jessica were staying at in Chicago. On my visits, I saw that our son was doing

OK, and I told his mother to make sure that nothing happened to him. Several weeks after Nate's death, just a few days before Thanksgiving, I called the house, and Jessica's stepmother answered. She told me that Jessica was in New Orleans working at a new job.

I dropped the phone; I could not believe it. The first thing that came to mind was that Jessica took Popi. Afraid, I asked the stepmother where Popi was, and she told me that Popi was at home with her boyfriend. She said that Jessica had left Chicago two weeks ago.

I got sick to my stomach and, saying nothing more, hung up the phone.

"Randy," I told my friend. "I need to get to Chicago now."

With no questions asked, we were on the highway. Within an hour, we were in Chicago, knocking down the door to Jessica's stepmother's house. I told Randy to grab the gun just in case she and her boyfriend tried to stop me--they never did care for me. Fortunately, nothing happened, and I was able to take Popi home. Jessica never even called about his whereabouts.

MAKING A CHANGE

It was time to start doing something different with my life. I learned quickly that Jessica was not going to a part of Popi's life, and he deserved a chance. I did not know how to give him a better life, however, because I knew nothing about being a father or a man. Many days and nights, I just did what I thought was best for him. I still had money and drugs on the streets, but I never collected it. Instead, I humbled myself to go to the public aid office to apply for a Link card. They gave it to me.

It was very difficult walking into the store to shop with a Link card. At this point in my life, I had no money, and I was at my lowest emotional and psychological state. Each night I cried because I wanted to go back to the streets. Still, I dropped the gang life, even though I had made a vow that I would never leave the gang.

I could not love myself, and I felt that I was losing the love I once had for my son. I was truly sick. I did not know how to survive without the streets. I had known the streets all of my life; the streets were a love that I had also lost. Denying myself access to my old life, I sat each day in the apartment on 7th Street that I had once shared with Jessica, and the bills piled up because I had no money to pay them. The landlord threatened to put my son and I out in the streets, and a few months later he did. We had nowhere to go.

After the eviction, I looked for work nearly every day, and in February, 1999, it finally paid off: I landed a job through a temp service on the night shift at Warner Lambert, the gum factory. They started me out with $6.15 an hour. I was humiliated--even more so when I got my first check. I thought they had made a mistake--I made this kind of money in less than five minutes dealing dope. After a while, I moved to another shift and met Tonya on the job; she worked in the same department.

I really did not like Tonya but she liked me, and we had sex together. Consequently, she let Popi and me move in with her and her roommate. Unfortunately, our relationship was only sexual; neither of us cared for the other in a deeper way. Shortly after I moved in with her, things got very bad between us, so bad that she would curse at me in front of my son. All we did was fight. In the meantime, I disliked my job and wanted to quit, but Tonya would not let me quit. She would not let my son and I stay with her for free, no matter how much sex we were having.

I finally decided that I had had enough: I was not willing to raise my son in such a hostile environment. Very tired of the player life and feeling emotionally neglected, I just wanted to be alone with my son. Then I met a man who would change my life forever.

I would always see him in the lunchroom. He would not say much but just wave at me when saw me. To be honest, I thought he may have been gay. One night while I was on the assembly line packing gum into boxes, he walked up to my machine. I thought to myself, "I really don't have time to talk to anyone. I just want to do my job and go home." He introduced himself as Timothy Green, and I barely looked up at him. He then said that God had sent him over to talk to me. As he spoke, I looked over at my watch and saw that I had been at work for a little over an hour. I thought to myself, "Shit! This is going to be a long night—especially if I have to spend it with this guy!"

He looked at me for a long time. "God sent me to you," he explained. "God told me that you have just

69

suffered a great loss. You have lost someone very close to you—someone closer to you than your own mother. "

At that moment, he got my attention. The gum began to fall to the floor, and Timothy hit the red button to stop the machine.

"I just lost my brother," I said.

"God has a calling on your life, Verne," he responded. "Your entire family needs you to stand."

I stared at him in disbelief. I could not stand on my own two feet; how was I going to be able to stand for my entire family?

Timothy saw my response but continued speaking, telling me about his church and inviting me to come to one of their services. I listened to him with doubt in my heart. Later during that shift, we met in the lunchroom, and he shared with me stories about what God had done for him in his life. As we talked, he told me that he had known my father and mother. He also said that the last time he saw my twin brother and me, we were about two years old.

We had fun that night talking, but I had serious reservations about going to his church. I had a big problem believing in God. Still, over the next seven months, he continued to work with me, bringing his bible to work and reading it to me, helping me to understand God's word.

One night in March while lying in bed with my son, I decided for the first time in a very long time to get on my knees and talk to God. I talked aloud, not knowing what to say, and I closed my eyes. It was very late, but I stayed on the floor before my bed, talking to God. While kneeling there, I began to see an image of two caskets: a big one and a little one. In my mind, I could see myself walking up to them. Upon reaching them, I could see that inside the caskets' velvet interiors lay my son and I.

I quickly opened my eyes, fearful and confused of what I saw. For a long while, I was silent. Then I started talking to God again, asking him to help me understand the meaning of this vision. At first, I thought my son and I were going to die soon, but as I continued talking to God, asking him questions, I saw an image of Popi and I playing at the park; I was swinging Popi by his arms.

Then I heard a voice as low as a whisper speak the words, "Now choose."

"God," I cried softly. "I want to live! I want my son to live!"

Inside of me, I could still feel the pain that I had been feeling for such a long time, but I began to feel better that night. I talked to God for hours; I even fell asleep on my knees.

About a month later, I was in my son's room picking up things when I saw Nate's clothes hanging on the bunk bed. Catching a whiff of his scent, I completely broke down.

"God, if you're real," I cried, "take this pain from me! I've tried drugs, sex, alcohol, anger, pride, lust, money, hate--nothing has taken it away! Lord, I'll serve you for the rest of my days if you just take the pain away!"

Within a moment which nearly scared me to death, my pain was gone.

Still, my struggle with God would not stop. Each day, it seemed, I had to fight to keep my head above water. Finally, on a Wednesday night, I decided to go to the church that Timothy talked about—Faith Temple Church in Rockford--and it was such a great experience that I felt at last I could stop running. For the first time in my life, I felt free. Perhaps life was going to get better for my son and myself, I thought. In time, our lives really did get better.

In June 1999, I gave my will and life over to Christ. I was fortunate enough to have a group of brothers supporting me throughout my journey. Also, during this time my friend J.R, who had become my best friend since Nate's death, decided to change the course of his life. J.R. and I both had a tough time adjusting to our new lives, but with the help and support from the brothers at the church, we went through this change with peace in our hearts.

My brother Tyrone, or Ghost, would occasionally come to church with me. I had really wanted him to change his life; I wished very much for him to stand strong with me. I asked him to do it in memory of our brothers Nate and Eli. I do believe that Tyrone tried his best to change, but this was not enough. On December 6, 2000, he was killed. It was more than a killing: it was an execution. Tyrone was shot twice in the head. To this day, his killers have not been found.

Tyrone wasn't my biological brother, but he seemed like a real brother to me. I did not go to his funeral, though. Sometimes even now I feel guilty about that, but at the time I could not bear to see my brother's body. Just when everything had been going so well, I lost another brother. Mama went to Tyrone's funeral, and she later commented on how badly he had been beaten; it appeared that most of his bones were broken.

Tyrone's death set me back a few steps, but it did not stop me. At this time, I was in the process of developing a strong spiritual foundation. Under the guidance of the pastor at Faith Temple Church, I had begun to grow both mentally and spiritually. Daily, I was learning how to become a man, a father, and a son. I was doing well for myself, and while I grieved over the loss of my brother, I took comfort in the fact that I had tried to help him before he died. I had really tried to show Tyrone there was a different, and better, way to live.

I continued working hard at becoming a good Christian man, and in June 2003, I was awarded full custody of Popi, which I had not been granted before, even though Popi had been living with me nearly all of his life, excepting for the month after Nate's death when Jessica cared for him. I had gone to three court hearings to try to gain custody, whereas Jessica did not go to any of them. Truthfully, the law is often not in favor of the father, even if the father is doing the right thing. As I began to realize this, I became disappointed in our legal system, which would not honor a man for doing what most young black men will not do. Still, I was delighted to at last be given full custody of my son.

Being granted full custody of Popi was not the only good thing I experienced after giving my life over to Christ. I also met a wonderful, church-going woman who was to become my best friend. The first time I saw Angela, we were in church doing a "meet and greet." I was talking to a friend I knew from the streets who had decided to change his life, too, when across the room I saw her. She was the most beautiful woman I had ever seen. Looking at her, I felt in my heart that this woman was to be my wife.

I leaned over to my friend and said, "That's my wife over there."

"Where?" he asked.

I pointed to her. "Over there," I said. "In the black flower dress."

My friend laughed. "Boy, that's the pastor's baby girl. Good luck with that one!"

Days went on, and I could not get this girl out of my head; I really needed to see her again. Angela was in college at Northern Illinois University at the time, so I did not get to see her as much as I would have liked. Still, when she was in town visiting her family, I was really happy. She was in love with Popi, who was seventeen months old, and she always wanted to play with him. I, in turn, loved talking to Angela about Popi. Angela was amazed that I was a single father caring for my son.

As time went on, Angela and I began to talk more openly about ourselves. Our friendship made a breakthrough the day we were at a local restaurant with other church members. J.R had gone to the buffet line and started talking with Angela, who was smiling widely. I sat at the table, hoping my boy was hooking me up.

J.R. returned minutes later, smiling.

"What did she say?" I asked him.

"Well, I told her that you really liked her," he said. He sat down at the table and started to sugar into his lemonade.

"And?"

J.R.'s eyes twinkled. "And she told me that she liked you, too."

After that night, J.R and I were invited to visit Angela at college. She was very much what I wanted in a woman. As our relationship evolved, my friends started to see a change in me, and my family did, too--but unlike my friends, they weren't happy or supportive of me. In fact, most of my relatives turned their backs on me.

I wish I could say our relationship worked, but on the contrary, life with Angela was difficult. We had so many plans for our future that did not happen. I tried to love her with all that I had in me, only finding in the process that I could not love myself. I tried to give and show my love to her, but I was to discover in the end that I had no real love to give.

I grew up not knowing how to love anyone or anything. My life was based on survival. Treated like shit my entire life, I had no faith in people. I thought that I wanted to love someone some day, but most of all what I really wanted was to be loved. Love is very hard to give if it is unconditional. Unconditional love is real love, unlike conditional love, the I'll-only-love-you-if-you-love-me type of love. A man who loves unconditionally is willing to lay down his life for those he loves; he doesn't lie, break promises, hurt people, or take lives. Unconditional love gives life to the lifeless. It gives hope. It is very compassionate—the man who loves unconditionally is genuinely concerned about his lover's well being. By the time I learned this, my relationship with Angela was over. It took four years to build what we had, but only a few minutes to tear it all down.

I once wrote a prose poem about it called "A Heart Was Broken Today."

Today I woke up to the electricity being off in my apartment due to the rainstorm last night. The morning was gloomy, even chilly, but for the more part comfortable. I got up and started my day with a tight trim across my face and a clean-cut shave to my head. Suddenly, the phone rang. "Who could this be?" I wondered, looking at the clock that read 8:22 a.m. I entered the kitchen to answer the phone. "Hello," I said. Well, what do you know--it was the love of my life. Yes, it was Angela. I spoke to her, feeling a bit nervous, thinking that something was wrong. I went on to tell her about my big day in court. "Today is the day I'll get full custody of Popi," I told her. She acted as though she hadn't heard me, showing no happiness for me. "I have to talk to you about something,"

I heard her say. My heart picked up a few beats as I sat in the chair and thought to myself, "This can't be good." She continued, "Our relationship is over." For a second, I lost my breath. Did she say that? Yes, she did, but why did she call to tell me this? Why today? At that moment, my heart knew exactly how the morning skies felt. I wanted to cry. Everything and everyone that I loved just seemed to walk out of my life. "What have I done wrong?" I asked her. "No! No! Don't say that," she said. "Well, why can't you tell me different?" I asked her. I still love her, but why? I still want to be with her. I can't live without her, and I don't understand. Hopefully, I will get an answer, but until then I have just another broken heart.

Angela took a job 800 miles away from Rockford. After she left, I thought about her from time to time. Sometimes I missed her. Eventually, I came to appreciate that throughout our relationship, she made me stronger.

GIVING BACK

During the time that I began regularly attending and participating in the events of Faith Temple Church, I understood that drug and alcohol abuse were destroying the lives of not only Rockford's youth but also the lives of the next generation, their children. I badly wanted to help in this area, but I did not know much about addiction. While I watched as nearly my entire family used drugs and alcohol, I did not understand why. I prayed that God would give me the opportunity and the ability to help the youth of my city.

While working for Rock River Ford, a man I had sold a car to asked me if I had ever thought about working with alcoholics and drug addicts. I told him, "No, not really."

He said, "Man, I know you will do well. We need a brother like you working with us."

At the time, I didn't really think too much about it because I didn't have a high school diploma or a GED; I hadn't needed either to work at the dealership. Still, I realized that I would not want to work forever at the dealership: my heart wasn't into selling cars. I took the customer's advice and applied for a job with Rockford M.E.L.D.

During my interview with the program's director, I was offered the job. The director then explained about the documents that I needed to bring in, including a high school diploma or GED.

"I don't have either," I told him.

The look on his face was of pure disappointment. He then took me into a small room, put his hands on my shoulders, looked me in the eyes, and said, "Man, Verne, you need to get your GED. It is something we encourage all young men and women to do." Embarrassed, I promised him that I was going to work hard to get it.

"Even if you don't get the job here," he told me, "get the GED because you're going to need it!"

Six and a half months after that conversation, in February 2005, I received my GED from Rock Valley

College. I felt very good about myself: this was a major accomplishment. Dropping out of school at the age of fifteen and going back at the age of thirty was one of the hardest things I had ever done, but I did it. I then applied for a position at Rosecrance Substance Abuse Treatment Center, and I got the job pretty much on the spot.

On April 11, 2005, I started my career at Rosecrance. Life was good: I had a great group of guys supporting me; I had nearly six years of living a clean life style; and my son Popi was doing well in school and sports. Still, even with all of these good things, I felt empty. At this time I had no one to share my life with, and eventually I grew depressed. Not only did I need a companion, but Popi needed a mother. He was getting older and wanted to know why his mother wasn't around.

I had prayed for years that God would one day bless me with a wife and my son with a mother, but in my heart I felt that I wasn't ready for a wife. There was still a great deal of hurt residing inside of me. On the outside, it may have looked as though I was all put together, but on the inside I was hurting. I didn't want to mess up someone's life because I was still messed up. The reality was that I felt conflicted emotions: part of me wanted to wait, and yet another part of me greatly desired a relationship to happen immediately.

The wait was long, but then I saw her; she was a new hire. I was working on some paper work when I spotted her walking down the hall with my boss. I was not able to see her face, but her walk was so sexy that I hoped she would get either the job or the intern shift. When my boss came back to my workstation, he introduced her to my co-workers and me. "Stephanie, uh that's cool," I thought.

A few days later, Stephanie was hired. She worked during the days while training, but she was hired for a second shift position. I also worked the second shift. After a few months, she would join me and another friend that I had met at work for dinner together, just the three of us. We would talk for hours, sometimes till one or two o'clock in the morning. After departing from each other, I would think about her. I could see myself hanging out with her. I found out later that Stephanie was in a relationship, but was about to end it.

While looking for a place to live, she and a friend came over to look at my apartment. It was then that I knew that I liked this girl. A few months later, our relationship progressed, but I was still dealing on an emotional basis with Angela, who had called a few times to ask if I was with another woman. I told her about Stephanie, and she was totally against it. She told me that I was moving too fast. I responded that Stephanie and I weren't dating;

I just really liked her. Angela got angry and cut the conversation short.

Angela was right, though. It was too early for me to begin a relationship with Stephanie. Later when I told Stephanie this, she wasn't happy. Nonetheless, I needing to see if I still had strong feelings for her, I took vacation time and headed to my cousin's house in Nashville, Tennessee. During this time, I avoided calling Stephanie, and I also started to gain a better perspective about myself: while I wasn't quite over Angela, I was able to move forward with my life. Then, after a period of praying and soul searching, asking myself if I was really ready to become emotionally involved with another woman again, I got my answer. In May 2006, Stephanie bought the book <u>The Color Purple</u> for my birthday. She knew that I was a big fan of the movie, but what stole my heart was what she wrote in the book. I will share her words:

V-

Happy Birthday!

I am so grateful for the time & opportunity I have had with you. Thank you for being (& remaining) you.

-Steph Fusinetti

*A few of the many reasons why I absolutely love your company.
-you challenge me.

-you hear what I have to say.
-you look at me when I talk.
-you fight for me.
-the way you look at me.
-the way you touch me.
-the way you kiss me.
-the way you smell.
-the way you smile at me.
-the way you scrunch your nose at me.
-the way you talk to me.
-you try to understand me.
-you accept me for who I am.
-you want what I have to offer you.
-the way you accept others.
-your compassion towards others.
-the fact that I can physically see that compassion.
-the goals you have for yourself.
-your love of family.
-where you have been.
-your openness to share with me.
-you make sense to me.
-you have found a comfortable home within my heart.
-you refuse to grow your hair out.
-you believe in yourself.
-you believe in others.
-you refuse to give in.
-your intense love of God.
-how no one can take your faith from you.
-you refuse to believe what is not true.
-your willingness.
-the way you hug me.
-you do not doubt my fears.

-you do not fear my doubts.
-you do not give into my assumptions.
-you cook!
-your love of culture.
-your "old school" traditions.
-your honesty.
-your ability to discover & embrace beauty.
-your ability to entrap me with mere words.

"And I love his dear eyes in which the vulnerability & beauty of his soul can be plainly read." From <u>The Color Purple</u> (238).

I share these words because in this poem, Stephanie showed me what I could not see about myself. She opened my eyes to see what kind of man I really am. I have never had anyone say those words to me.

In 2007, Stephanie and I were engaged. It was a great moment for me. However, her family thought she was making a big mistake. Not only did her family think this, but mine was also unhappy about our engagement. After only a few months, we called off our engagement. Stephanie moved from the apartment we had shared, and I moved into a friend's home. I was hurt by our break up, for awhile I believed that I was a good man, I thought that Stephanie would not give me a chance to prove this. I thought that Stephanie did not want to commit to me because she believed I was still a "player." It was true that other women would flirt with me, and sometimes I would return the attention, but my heart was all for Stephanie. In the time after our break up, I would drive to her apartment building in the late hours of the night and park in front, wanting to knock on her door. My pride would not let me do it.

Work was also hard for the both of us, for we worked in the same building. I knew that I wanted my life to be with her, but I still had some private issues to resolve before I could become the husband that I desired to be. I used this time apart from Stephanie to work continually on myself from the inside. Change did not come easily, but I was determined. I was never a foolish man, I thought, although I had to admit that I had done an endless amount of foolish things in my life. My heart told me that Stephanie was a magnificent woman and that I should not allow another man to have her. I prayed that God would make me the man that she needed. Fortunately, God did just that.

On October 25, 2008, Stephanie and I were married; it was second happiest day of my life. She was so beautiful on our wedding day that even to this day I love looking at our wedding photo. Truly, she grows on me each day; she is that "second wind" that keeps me living. Not only has Stephanie been a wonderful wife, but she has been an awesome mother for Popi. Popi has now grown to be a handsome young man, and he tells me often that I am his "hero." Those words are priceless to me.

Two weeks before Stephanie and I were to be wed, we discovered that she was pregnant, and about four months after our wedding, we got the news that we were going to have a daughter. Wow! No words could begin to describe the joy in my heart when I learned this news.

On June 5, 2009, Celicia Nevaeh Johnson (Celie) was born a very healthy 7lb, 6oz. She is a great addition to our family!

THE PRESENT

As I look back on my life, I can truly say I have come a long way. Still, I have a ways to go. I have shared the story of my life because I believe it can help those who face the same situations I have faced. I have told others, including myself, that my life has not always been fair, but it has been "even", meaning that for everything I have done right or wrong, I have reaped both the benefits and the consequences. In other words, I have reaped what I sowed. My family did not know how to live a God-fearing life, and as a consequence, they lived a dysfunctional life. Who is to blame here?

The way I see it, each of us has been given in life a hand of cards to play. Even when we make bad decisions, it really does not define who we are. Most of us are good people on the inside, but we lose this goodness when we are forced to play the game of survival on the streets. My mama abused drugs, and my father is spending his entire life on Death Row. The decisions they made ultimately affected their futures, as is the case with us all.

It wasn't until I turned twenty-four that I needed to know the truth about myself. It was then that I started to ask myself a lot of questions, like "Who am I?" "Why am I on this earth?" "What is my purpose in life?" As a kid, however, I was a dreamer: I lived in a world that only existed in my mind. I turned to a fantasy world to escape the hurt and pain caused by my upbringing. I grew up not being able to work through, or with, my emotions, and the pain I felt crippled me.

Eventually, I came to believe that the world was against me. By the time I reached adulthood, I was afraid to get involved in any type of a relationship because I felt had too much baggage in my life to contend with. Keeping apart from people, not wanting to hurt anyone, I grew lonely. With loneliness came depression, and as I got depressed, my isolation from others became more pronounced.

After a while, my family was hurt by what they saw as my rejection of them, and they did not want anything to do with me. They thought I felt I was better than them.

That was not the case at all; I just wanted to get my life in order for Popi's sake. He was the first person in my life who gave me the hope that I needed to move forward.

I only began helping myself when I began helping others. At first, I volunteered my time to feed the homeless, and later I got involved with Faith Temple Church. The pastor at Faith Temple taught me how to be a man. He showed me how to do things that I did not think possible for a man to do, like be a father to his children, or love his wife as Christ loved the church. He taught me morals and values that I will hold dear for the rest of my life. Without him, there would be no me.

The pastor also showed me that the hardest thing I will ever do in my life is change. To completely change the man that I had been was, and still is, a difficult task. In the process of changing myself, I have learned that the decisions I make have everything to do with the outcome of my life. My mother, father, brothers, sisters, friends, wife, and children have all played a role in making me who I am, but it is I who determines what I become.

I have worked hard to do the right things in life so my children won't grow up filled with hate and confusion. I know I cannot protect them from all the evil in this world, but I can teach them to love one other and to respect those who have authority over them. Daily, I strive to instill in my children love of their parents and grandparents, and I encourage them to make education their number one priority. Through the grace of God and the support of family and friends, I was able to turn my back on the life style that destroyed those I loved, and that nearly destroyed me. At times, I still think about having that dance with death, but I trust that God will keep me safe in his arms. The biggest enemy I have ever fought in my life was the man in the mirror, and there were no one standing behind me.